D1123414

EXPLORING THE WORLD OF

Coyotes

Tracy C. Read

FIREFLY BOOKS

Published by Firefly Books Ltd. 2011

First Printing

Publisher Cataloging-in-Publication Data (U.S.)
Read, Tracy C.
Exploring the world of coyotes / Tracy C. Read.
[ ] p. : photos. ; cm.
Includes index.
ISBN-13: 978-1-55407-795-3 (bound)
ISBN-10: 1-55407-795-8 (bound)
ISBN-13: 978-1-55407-796-0 (pbk.)
ISBN-10: 1-55407-796-6 (pbk.)
1. Coyote -- Juvenile literature. I. Title.
599.77/25 dc22 QL737.C22R433 2011

Library and Archives Canada Cataloguing in Publication
Read, Tracy C.
Exploring the world of coyotes / Tracy C. Read.
Includes index.
ISBN-13: 978-1-55407-795-3 (bound)
ISBN-10: 1-55407-795-8 (bound)
ISBN-13: 978-1-55407-796-0 (pbk.)
ISBN-10: 1-55407-796-6 (pbk.)
1. Coyote--Juvenile literature. I. Title.
QL737.C22R418 2011 j599.77'25
C2010-907683-4

Published in the United States by
Firefly Books (U.S.) Inc.
P.O. Box 1338, Ellicott Station
Buffalo, New York 14205

Published in Canada by
Firefly Books Ltd.
66 Leek Crescent
Richmond Hill, Ontario L4B 1H1

The publisher gratefully acknowledges the financial support for our publishing program by the Government of Canada through the Canada Book Fund as administered by the Department of Canadian Heritage.

Cover and interior design by
Janice McLean, Bookmakers Press Inc.

Manufactured by Printplus Limited in Shen Zhen, Guang Dong, P.R.China in January, 2011, Job #S101200438.

Front cover: © Masterfile Royalty Free
Back cover: © Dennis Donohue/Shutterstock
Back cover, inset, left: © Wayne Lynch
Back cover, inset, right top: © Richard Seeley/Shutterstock
Back cover, inset, right bottom: © Tom Tietz/iStockphoto

CONTENTS

CANINE CUDDLING

Sniffing, licking, nuzzling, nudging — it's all part of getting to know each other, coyote-style.

MEET THE COYOTE

With its narrow face, elongated nose, pointed ears and grizzled fur, the coyote bears a strong resemblance to its canid cousin, the gray wolf. In fact, Native Americans called this slimmer, trimmer model "little wolf." Other common names include prairie wolf and brush wolf.

Like the wolf, the coyote (*Canis latrans*) has had a long, violent history with the Europeans who settled in North America and who regarded wolves and coyotes as a threat to their livestock and game. In fact, campaigns to eliminate the wolf were so successful that only small populations have survived.

The wolf's loss, however, has been the coyote's gain. Its original stomping ground in North America was the midwestern prairies and grasslands, where it wisely steered clear of its fiercer, stronger canine relative. But as wolf numbers declined, the coyote quickly moved in to fill the gap. And while this wild dog has likewise been shot at, poisoned and trapped, it has dramatically expanded its range and now lives throughout most of Canada, the United States and Central America, in rural, urban and suburban settings.

Constantly adjusting its habitat, diet, mating habits and hunting style, the wily coyote refuses to fade away. For its remarkable talent to beat the odds, wildlife photographer/writer Erwin Bauer called the coyote a "super dog."

OLD DOG, NEW TRICKS

A master in the art of survival, the coyote tirelessly adapts to life in a hostile world. Today, there are probably more coyotes in North America than at any other time in history.

ANATOMY LESSON

Smaller than the gray wolf, larger than the red fox and roughly the same size as the red wolf, the medium-sized coyote is also a member of the dog family, Canidae.

As we've noted, this wild canid has lots in common with its relatives, but a few traits make it distinct. For instance, the coyote's perky, oversized ears and big bushy tail, often tipped in black and typically held low between its hind legs, set it apart from both the wolf and the German shepherd, which it also resembles, as do its long, slender legs and its feet. And its feet are relatively small compared with the sturdy, big-footed wolf. In addition, the coyote's nose is narrower and more pointed than the wolf's, and the nose pad is smaller.

There are 19 subgroupings of *Canis latrans*, and members vary in size and appearance depending on where they live. The adult male is almost always bigger and heavier than the female. The fur of the lightweight desert-dwelling coyote can be a dull brownish yellow, tan and/or red in color. In the north, the coyote's fur tends to be grizzled and black and is longer and coarser, offering the animal better insulation in winter. The fur on the belly and throat of all coyotes is lighter in color.

In late spring or summer, the coyote starts to shed its fur, replacing it with a shorter, cooler coat for the warmer weather.

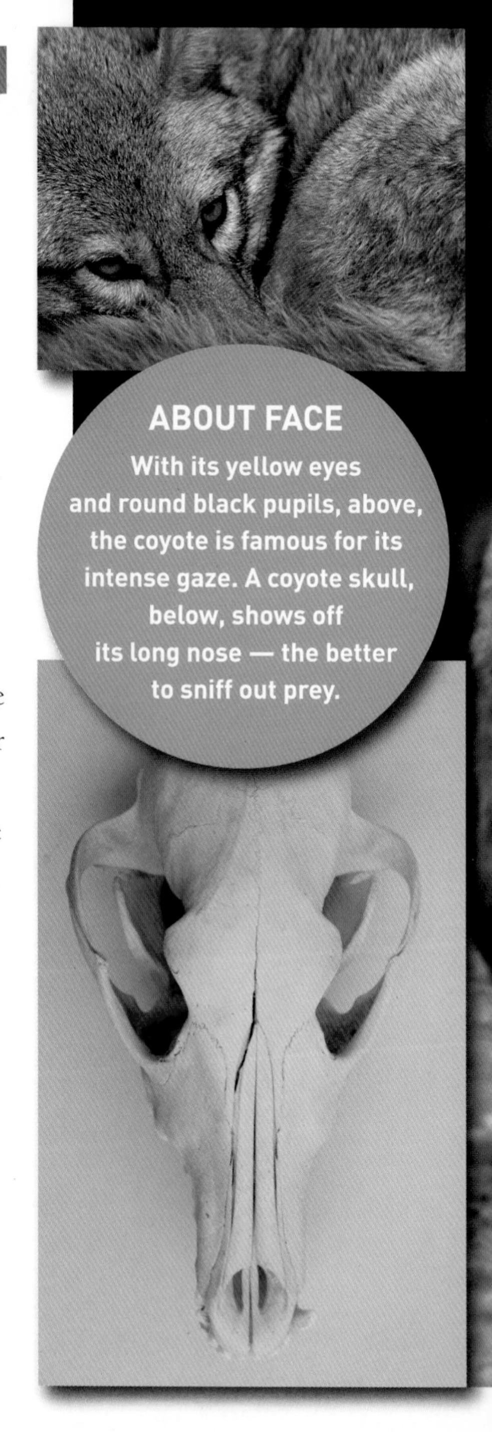

ABOUT FACE

With its yellow eyes and round black pupils, above, the coyote is famous for its intense gaze. A coyote skull, below, shows off its long nose — the better to sniff out prey.

A LONG, LEAN RUNNING MACHINE

This wild dog can tucker out its prey by running at 25 miles per hour (40 km/h) for extended periods, and it can hit 40 miles per hour (65 km/h) in a burst of speed when needed.

COYOTE FACTS

While not the most powerful predator in the wild, the coyote uses speed, agility and hyper attention to details to survive.

Ears
Funnel-shaped and erect, the coyote's ears are acutely sensitive.

Eyes
Intense yellow eyes with round black pupils give the coyote a look of cunning.

Teeth
The coyote has 42 teeth, including four extra-long, extra-sharp canines that it uses to puncture the throat of its prey.

Paws
The coyote's claws are typically worn down by constant movement and are not used to attack prey.

Length
From nose to tail tip, the coyote measures 3½ to 5 feet (107-153 cm).

Fur
Coarse guard hairs over a dense undercoat keep the coyote warm in winter.

Tail
Measuring from 11½ to 15½ inches (29-40 cm) long, the coyote's tail is full and bushy and may be held horizontally to show aggression.

Height
On average, a coyote is 18 to 24 inches (46-61 cm) high at the shoulder.

Weight
The average weight of the male coyote is 18 to 50 pounds (8-23 kg); the female is 15 to 40 pounds (7-18 kg).

TENDERFOOT

With its long legs and nimble paws, this lean coyote makes its way along an old fence rail, its big ears on the alert for the sound of a small rodent rustling in the dry grass.

NATURAL TALENTS

Hunted by generations of humans who've made an industry out of coyote killing, the coyote has had little choice but to live its life on the defensive. Yet in spite of its long-standing status as Public Enemy #1, this wild dog has impressively managed to beat the odds. What qualities does the coyote count on to live another day?

A major weapon in the coyote's survival arsenal is its ability to quickly spot would-be predators and potential prey. Armed with eyesight that allows it to distinguish a range of shapes and movements under most lighting conditions, including the low light at dusk and dawn, the coyote constantly scans its surroundings for danger as well as opportunity.

An exceptional sense of hearing works hand in hand with the coyote's superior vision to help keep it safe. Its large, triangular ears direct the faintest of sounds to the coyote's inner ear for identification — from the rustling of a mouse in the distant dry grass to the footfall of an approaching intruder or hunter.

A quick look at the coyote's face reveals one of this animal's other main strengths: Its long, narrow nose is designed to gather information, picking up the scent of creatures, both living and dead — either are possible meals for this omnivore.

Observers have seen the coyote suddenly change direction,

WILY COYOTE

Eyes front and center, ears cocked and ready, these coyotes do their best to eliminate the element of surprise.

NOW YOU SEE ME

The rodent-loving coyote prepares to go deep for a vole scurrying beneath its feet.

apparently to avoid something it has smelled or heard that it perceives as a threat. Indeed, this wild dog is famously cautious. It does not take unnecessary risks if it can help it.

While its wide-ranging menu illustrates that the coyote doesn't have well-developed taste buds, it does prove that a full stomach ranks very high on the coyote's list of needs. Its willingness to make do with what is on hand is just one of the adaptable coyote's trademark traits.

But perhaps more important than all the physical strengths and skills the coyote brings to its daily life is its sheer determination to keep on going. Tough and resourceful, this wild animal clearly does not consider surrender an option, though avoiding confrontation rather than engaging in battle is the coyote's way. If there is a route over or around an obstacle, the coyote will find it. Unfortunately for the coyote, that makes it an irresistible challenge to hunters everywhere.

COYOTE HUNGRY

This desert denizen has its ears and nose to the wind, listening and smelling for signs of its next meal.

SIGHT
The coyote can see more detail in a landscape than most other animals or humans.
HEARING
Large ears help the coyote gather up faint sounds, the better to detect its prey.
SMELL
The coyote's keen sense of smell allows it to find a meal even under deep snow.
TASTE
A coyote's favorite nibbles could be vegetable, animal and, occasionally, mineral.
TOUCH
Nuzzling and other displays of affection are part of the coyote's courtship ritual.

FAMILY DYNAMIC

By the time a female coyote is about two years old and the male is three, family life is on their minds. For the female, however, choosing a mate is far from a snap decision.

In early winter, several males gather around the female, showing off their strengths and skills. For two to three months, the female considers the competition, at last picking the male that has made the best impression. This pair forms a bond that is often lifelong and is the heart of the coyote's social structure. Mating usually takes place in February.

Like wolves, coyotes often live in groups called packs that are led by an "alpha couple." In addition to the alpha couple, the pack may include members of an earlier generation of offspring. These young coyotes help the parents feed and rear the new pups.

After mating, the female scouts out a safe location for a place in which to give birth. With the help of the male, she may dig a den along a stream bank or in a sandy hill. Other den options include a hollowed-out log or the abandoned den of another animal. About two months later, a litter of four to seven pups is born.

While the mother sticks close to home to nurse her young and regain her strength after giving birth, the male and other pack members bring her food. The pups' eyes open at two weeks, and by three weeks, their teeth

PLAYTIME FOR PUPS

Coyotes of all ages play with their packmates, sometimes introducing a physical object into the game.

have come in and they begin to eat meat. They're also ready to venture just outside the den entrance, gaining experience and confidence with each outing. Coyote pups are known to be vicious with their littermates — these pups fight for real, quickly showing their siblings who's boss.

Now the pups' real education begins. Pack members offer the young coyotes increasingly bigger animals that have already been killed, and the pups learn to identify the food groups on the coyote menu. Soon they're presented with living prey, on which they practice and learn to kill. And shortly after that, they join their parents and siblings on hunting trips.

Life for the youngsters is just as tough as it is for the adults. There's a good chance that only two of the pups will survive the summer. Disease, predators and lack of food are all threats. By fall, one pup may be sent out on its own, while its mate remains to help the alpha couple through the next breeding cycle.

PECKING ORDER
A parent shows a pup who's boss, above, while one sibling submits to another's show of strength, below.

DEN SECURITY

Coyote mothers are extremely shy about sharing their address, especially with humans, and will move their pups at the first sign that their location has been discovered.

CALL OF THE WILD

As the coyote has moved closer to our communities, its dusk-to-dawn vocalizations have become a familiar sound to more and more people. For some, the coyote's howls are an ominous reminder that a predator lurks at the edge of their lives. For others, the haunting song of the coyote is the voice of the wilderness at its purest.

The coyote communicates in several ways, and we can only speculate about the meaning of each. Like most animals, it probably uses sound to warn and send information to its pack and to challenge strangers in its territory. Its repertoire ranges from barking, growling, whimpering and whining to yipping, yapping and high-pitched howling. The sounds may be joyful, but they can also signal stress or threat.

In addition, the coyote communicates through its steely stare, by the position of its ears, head and tail and by curling its lips and baring its teeth.

As with other members of the dog family, the coyote leaves telltale evidence of its presence around its territory in the form of scent markings. These are released from various glands or in small amounts of urine. It's a nose-driven system that signals "I was here" to friends and foe. The markings also alert outsiders that the territory is defended and that they should steer clear, often saving the coyote from energy-sapping battles over limited resources.

COYOTE CHORUS

The coyote's lonely voice carries across great distances, and even when only two coyotes are vocalizing, it sounds like a pack. Like the wolf, the coyote may howl alone, but once it starts, other coyotes quickly join in.

THE KEY TO SUCCESS

Every day, dozens of animal species become extinct all over the world, usually as a result of habitat loss due to human activities. But in the century-old grudge match between humans and coyotes, the coyote has been declared "the winna!" Its knock-out punch? The ability to change.

When humans make life intolerable, the coyote simply moves to a new address. When its food source is eliminated, this omnivore finds something different for dinner. If it can't feed its offspring, it takes a break from reproducing.

As a result, a creature that once patrolled North America's mid-western grasslands now lives throughout the continent — in deserts, forests, woodlands, marshes and foothills and near farms and ranches, where it has access to small livestock. And like its cousin, the red fox, the coyote has turned the tables by migrating to human communities. Today, it is not uncommon to see a coyote trotting along a city side street or at a local park.

Like other wild dogs, the coyote makes its living on a piece of land called a territory. The size of its territory is mostly determined by the coyote's ability to feed itself within its borders. When prey is plentiful, its territory covers roughly 40 to 50 square miles (100-130 sq km). If the hunting is poor, it might be twice as big.

Wildlife photographer Erwin Bauer compared the coyote's

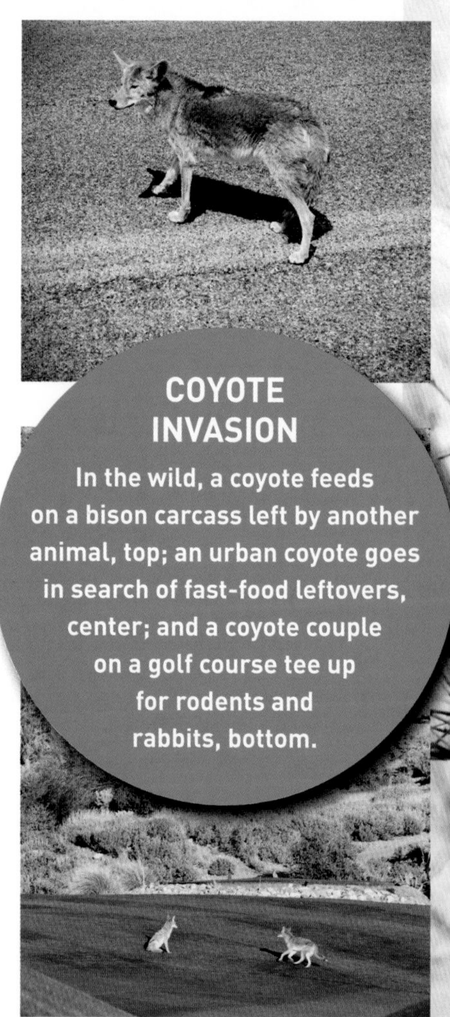

COYOTE INVASION

In the wild, a coyote feeds on a bison carcass left by another animal, top; an urban coyote goes in search of fast-food leftovers, center; and a coyote couple on a golf course tee up for rodents and rabbits, bottom.

SNACK ATTACK

After detecting a vole beneath the snow, this coyote shows off a classic catlike pounce.

foraging habits to those of "a smart supermarket shopper always looking for the best bargains." Indeed, the coyote enjoys whatever is in season or on offer.

While the wolf hunts in a pack to increase its success at killing large animals, the coyote often works solo, dining on items that are easily found and caught by the solitary hunter. By stalking and pouncing on rodents and by locating, then rushing small mammals like rabbits and ground squirrels, the coyote meets roughly half its nutritional needs. But as it crisscrosses its range, it also feeds on birds, insects, snakes, berries and fruit.

The coyote's reputation for creative problem solving is never more obvious than in its hunting strategies. Coyotes have been seen fishing for crayfish and carp; following vultures to get their share of dead flesh; and teaming up with a partner to hunt prairie dogs, with one distracting the prey while the other attacks.

In a rare wildlife partnership, the coyote and badger, also a meat-eater, sometimes join forces to flush ground squirrels from their burrows. As the badger digs into the burrow, the coyote stands by a side entrance to snatch up a fleeing squirrel.

Bad weather, disease, predators, an uncertain food supply — the super dog has stared these threats down and emerged victorious, a wildlife lesson in how to survive.

PET DETECTOR

As coyotes boldly settle into life in the suburbs, the easy pickings of a kitty dozing on a deck may be irresistible. Pet owners in coyote country are urged to remember: It's a dog-eat-cat world out there, so keep your furry companion in the house or risk its untimely end.

WHAT'S ON THE MENU?

Items too numerous to list have been found in the bellies of coyotes, from snails, reptiles, insects, fish and birds to leather boots and tin cans. Still, roughly 90 percent of this wild dog's food source comes from small rodents, such as mice and ground squirrels, midsized rabbits and larger fare like sheep and deer. The coyote takes its meat dead or alive but rounds out its menu with a variety of fruits and berries.

MOUTH TRAP

Success. The coyote's lightning speed has ended badly for an unlucky rodent.

PHOTOS © SHUTTERSTOCK
p. 3 Richard Seeley
p. 5 Sascha Burkard
p. 6 bottom: Tom Smith
p. 7 Ron Hilton
p. 8 B.G. Smith
p. 9 Tony Campbell
p. 12 Harris Shiffman
p. 13 Holly Kuchera
p. 18 top: Richard Seeley
p. 21 Quintin Slade
p. 22 top: Murat Subatli
p. 22 berries: mmattner
p. 22 prairie dog: Darrell J. Rohl
p. 23 top: Richard Seeley
p. 23 eggs: Stephanie Frey
p. 23 skink: Ryan M. Bolton
p. 23 field mouse: Mircea Bezergheanu
p. 23 cottontail rabbit: Ron Rowan Photography
p. 23 white-tail deer: B.G. Smith

PHOTOS © ISTOCKPHOTO
p. 10 top: Todd Burton
p. 15 Tom Tietz
p. 17 Ben Renard-Wiart
p. 18 top: David Parsons
p. 20 middle: archives
p. 20 bottom: Denny Medley

PHOTOS © TIM FITZHARRIS
p. 6 top
p. 11
p. 18 bottom
p. 20 top

PHOTOS © WAYNE LYNCH
p. 10 bottom
p. 16 top and bottom
p. 22 bottom left